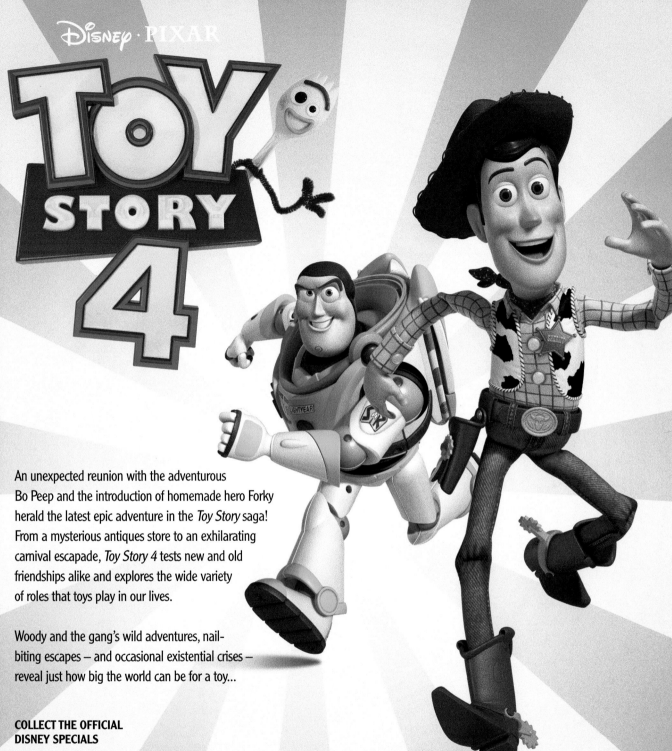

DISNEY · PIXAR

TOY STORY 4

An unexpected reunion with the adventurous Bo Peep and the introduction of homemade hero Forky herald the latest epic adventure in the *Toy Story* saga! From a mysterious antiques store to an exhilarating carnival escapade, *Toy Story 4* tests new and old friendships alike and explores the wide variety of roles that toys play in our lives.

Woody and the gang's wild adventures, nail-biting escapes – and occasional existential crises – reveal just how big the world can be for a toy...

COLLECT THE OFFICIAL DISNEY SPECIALS

Dumbo
The Lion King (July 2019)
Frozen 2 (October 2019)
Artemis Fowl (2020)

TOY STORY 4:
The Official Movie Special
ISBN: 9781787731820
First published June 2019

DISTRIBUTION
US Newsstand: Total Publisher Services, Inc.
John Dziewiatkowski. 630-851-7683
US Newsstand Distribution: Curtis Circulation Company
US Bookstore Distribution: The News Group
US Direct Sales Market: Diamond Comic Distributors

For info on advertising contact adinfo@titanemail.com

Printed in the US by Quad.

Titan Authorized User. No part of this publication may be reproduced, stored in a retrival system, or transmitted, in any form or by any means, without the prior written permission of the publisher.

DISNEY PUBLISHING WORLDWIDE
Global Magazines, Comics and Partworks Publisher: Lynn Waggoner. Editorial Team: Bianca Coletti (Director, Magazines), Guido Frazzini (Director, Comics), Stefano Ambrosio (Executive Editor, New IP), Carlotta Quattrocolo (Executive Editor), Camilla Vedove (Senior Manager, Editorial Development), Behnoosh Khalili (Senior Editor), Julie Dorris (Senior Editor), Mina Riazi (Assistant Editor), Jonathan Manning (Assistant Editor). Design: Enrico Soave (Senior Designer).
Art: Ken Shue (VP, Global Art), Roberto Santillo (Creative Director), Marco Ghiglione (Creative Manager), Manny Mederos (Senior Illustration Manager), Stefano Attardi (Illustration Manager). Portfolio Management: Olivia Ciancarelli (Director). Business & Marketing: Mariantonietta Galla (Senior Manager, Franchise), Virpi Korhonen (Editorial Manager).

Thank you to Christopher Troise, Shiho Tilley, Eugene Paraszczuk and all at Disney.

Titan
MAGAZINES

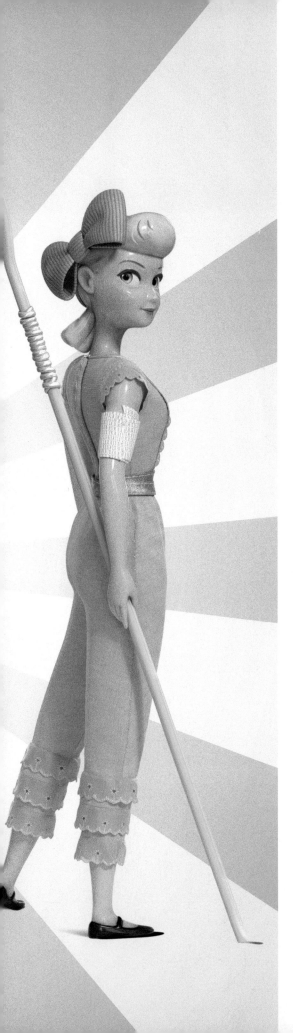

CONTENTS

JOSH COOLEY

Toy Story 4's director, Josh Cooley, shares his excitement at working on the movie – but which character did he relate to more: Woody, Buzz, or Forky?

While Josh Cooley has assembled an impressive list of Pixar film credits over the past 15 years – from storyboard artist on *The Incredibles*, *Cars*, and *Up*, to story supervisor on *Inside Out* – *Toy Story 4* marks his first time in the director's chair on a feature-length animated film. But as he explains, he was able to channel his experiences into making the next chapter of Woody and the gang's story...

Toy Story 4: The Official Movie Special: There was a sense of finality with *Toy Story 3*; how did you approach this next chapter in the *Toy Story* story?

Josh Cooley: It was important that it felt like this movie wasn't just another adventure. It had to have meaning to it, so that it felt as important as the last one. I knew that there had to be a major change in Woody, and I used the fact that I was in this whole new position [as a first-time feature director] and the way I was feeling as inspiration for Woody being in a whole new room – a whole new position – as well. My questions and insecurity and not knowing quite how it was all going to develop were my inspiration.

It wasn't until we started crafting it and things started to land that my wife pointed to Forky – who feels like he doesn't belong and doesn't know what's going on – and said, "You know that's you, right?"

When you looked back at the first three films, what did you glean from those in terms of what the core of this film should be?

It's just Woody's character. Every film is him learning something new and developing as a character. I watched the first three hundreds of times in a row to see the development, to capture the arc of the character and see where he's headed. How do we push his character, but also honor where he's been, and not make it feel like we're retreading anything that's been done before?

Three films in, we know these characters pretty well now. How do you keep things fresh?

I think that the new locations help immensely. Every film goes outside of the kids' rooms, but we really tried to expand the world as much as possible – going outside of the tri-county area; going to places where toys are that we've never been before, and seeing different types of toys that we've never seen. Making the world feel bigger was really important.

How did the story of *Toy Story 4* develop?

What really got me interested in this idea from the get-go was Woody being there within the new room with a new kid with new toys – a whole new dynamic. This is

01

02

01. Woody has a whole new adventure in *Toy Story 4*

02. Bonnie with her new BFF

03. Josh Cooley about Bo Peep in the previous films: "She gives [Woody] advice and is a reality check for him."

"The thing that makes Forky so much fun is that he's never seen any of the other *Toy Story* movies, so he doesn't understand the rules of the world."

04

> ## "My questions and insecurity [as a director] and not knowing quite how it was all going to develop were inspiration."

04. Bonnie faces her own challenges in *Toy Story 4* as she heads to "big kid school"

05. Woody with Forky – a character who literally comes to life in *Toy Story 4*

06. Gabby Gabby captures Forky

07. Bo tells Woody about the challenges she has faced

something we've never seen this character go through. Every kid is going to be different – my daughter plays differently with her toys than my son does – so I knew that with Bonnie, we couldn't just repeat the same story that Woody's the favorite toy; it had to be different. But Woody still has the same mindset of being there for her, no matter what. So, that's where the classroom idea came from: even though it's against the rules, he's going to stick to his guns and do with Bonnie what he's done for Andy. It works for a second, but then a problem rises out of that with Forky coming to life.

Then we set up the road trip to get him even more outside of his comfort zone. In the previous movies, we've implied that he's gone to cowboy camp with Andy, but we've never seen that. Cowboy camp could be right down the street for all we know. But to really see him outside of the tri-county area, outside of anything we've seen before, and actually get him away from everybody else… There's a great shot when he falls out of the RV and he's alone at nighttime in the wilderness. The first time I saw that, I realized we've never seen anything like that before with him. He's completely alone, not around anybody. That was really exciting to see something different like that.

How does Bonnie's situation help drive the story?
The same way that's it's a transition for Woody, I'd say it's a transition for Bonnie. She's going from preschool to kindergarten – you know, big kid school – so there's always

anxiety with that. It's something that everybody can relate to, whether it's changing jobs or just change in general; and being that Woody's gone through this before with Andy, he has an outlook that's different from all the other toys. His past with Andy, his experience with Andy is what he's bringing to the table to help her get through that. He's seen it before.

When they get to kindergarten orientation day, and Bonnie's having a hard time, how does Woody try to solve the problem?
He is the protective parent that I know I was when I was first dropping my kids off at school – you just want to keep looking through the window as you're supposed to be walking away. So we really wanted to have that feeling come across: that he's watching over her, protecting her, wanting to be there for her, wanting to do everything for her. When she gets slighted in class by kids unknowingly taking craft supplies away from her, and she starts to cry, that's the thing that tips Woody over the edge. He has to do something. He leaves the backpack and goes to the trash can to find the supplies that were taken from her, grabs some garbage in the process and returns it to her, and she creates Forky out of that trash.

What was the process of creating Forky as a character?
I remember we were joking in the story room about what would happen if we had a toy that was not manufactured. Would it be alive? It was just one of those weird existential questions in the *Toy Story* universe that are really fun to play around with. We weren't really thinking this would go anywhere; it was just an idea. We kept riffing off of it and it became, well, why not? Anything that kids play with, we can say has life. So, we just decided, let's have a character come to life.

The thing that makes Forky so much fun is he's never seen any of the other *Toy Story* movies, so he doesn't understand the rules of the world. I felt that to have a character who does not know the rules, and who we the audience are ahead of, was a great way to make a fourth movie feel fresh. We know what he's supposed to be, what he's supposed to act like, but he doesn't play by those rules at all. So, he can question anything, he can do whatever he wants, and that makes life hard for Woody.

Given your comments about Woody and some of the other characters, it seems one of the major themes in this film is change.

Yeah, all these characters are going through change, or have gone through change. The big thing coming into this was Woody has to change; he has to go through something and he can't just come out the other side the same character. The same thing with all those characters: Gabby Gabby is stuck there; Duke Caboom is kind of stuck as well; Forky is being forced to change; Woody has already gone through a change, and will change at the end.

Is it a theme you relate to personally?

The big thing for me, in a more global sense, is I'm not a big fan of change, which I think is probably a universal thing. Change has to happen, there's nothing you can do to stop it – it's just the way life is. I have young kids and I'm really enjoying this age of them right now, and I don't want that to stop. But I know it's going to, and things will change. Then being asked to direct the film was a huge change, not just in my career but my life as well, just how to approach everything. So, working through that was very similar to Woody. ■

WOODY

Sheriff Woody Pride returns in *Toy Story 4* as he is reunited with an old flame and mentors a nervous new toy…

T he brave and resourceful leader of the toys from Andy's bedroom, Woody's character has been defined by his relationship to Buzz Lightyear as the two have embarked on numerous adventures. However, *Toy Story 4* presents a different side of Woody...

AXEL GEDDES, FILM EDITOR

What have been the biggest challenges you faced during the making of Toy Story 4?

When we decided that we were going to make another *Toy Story* movie, the challenge was trying to figure out a way to give Woody another big lesson to learn, another arc to have so it didn't feel overdone.

Each [in-progress] screening is almost like a new version of the movie. In the two and a half years I've been here we've had eight screenings and each one will be a different version of the movie. It's almost like having cut eight movies. Each time saying, "Is this the arc that we want? Is this the lesson that Woody is going to learn? Is it a big enough one? Does it feel unique? Does it feel like something you already learned in *Toy Story* 3? Or does it feel like something we already went over?"

JOSH COOLEY, DIRECTOR

Were there particular elements of Woody's story from the first three films that you started from in terms of mapping out his next steps?

All of them add up, in a sense. In the first film it was, it's not just about you, it's about others – about not being the top dog in the spotlight in order to help others. Then him realizing that he's not going to live forever, and he'd rather be with his friends and family as opposed to just being a thing in a collector's case. Then being able to let go of Andy, and not to be there for kids in a selfish sense, but to be there for all kids, in a way.

Did Tom Hanks have a strong opinion on what he wanted for Woody?

I would rely on his opinion, because he does know this character so well. One of the most nerve-racking moments I had on this film was the first time I met with him, with this new idea. He said exactly what everyone's thinking: "Okay, why are we doing this?" I started to pitch him the film, and I got right to the classroom scene. I pitched him that, and he was like, "All right, you got me." That took a huge weight off me, just knowing that Tom Hanks was invested – that Woody's invested in this story now.

He knows the character so well. He would come up with ideas that either he would sell and make work, or we would workshop things in the room and come up with alternate ways to get that information or that feeling across. I don't think Woody would work without Tom Hanks at all, because he is

"I was made to help a child, I don't remember it being this hard." — Woody

01

02

03

01. Woody and his fellow toys join forces once again

02. Woody and Bo work together to save a toy in trouble

03. Tom Hanks' intimate knowledge of Woody led to the actor coming up with his own ideas of the character

04. A toy on a mission, Woody has a renewed sense of purpose

such a fearful character that Tom sells in such a loveable way.

We had three or four sessions where we had Annie [Potts, who voices Bo] and Tom together. They've known each other for such a long time, not just through *Toy Story* but I think their kids are friends as well. Having them together, there was a natural chemistry between the two of them which made it so much easier.

Does Forky give Woody a sense of purpose?

It gives him a renewed purpose of, "If I can't be there for my kids, here's the way that I can be, through Forky. I can help him understand his importance for Bonnie." That gives him a renewed sense of a job to do.

Is Woody and Forky's relationship akin to that of a parent-child?

Absolutely. We treated Forky as innocent as possible. It's fun to have an innocent character that knows nothing, and also has no confidence in anything that they're saying or thinking. There's a complete blank slate. He's been programmed to finish his purpose as a spork and not as a toy, so it's an instant conflict, in that Woody is the perfect toy, knows everything about being a toy, and has to teach a spork what that means, which is fantastic.

Did you draw upon your own life as a parent during the production process?

Absolutely! One of the best lines of the movie was written by Andrew Stanton. It's when Woody's holding Forky and he's describing basically what it means to be an empty nester. Only Andrew could have written that, because it's exactly what he's going through and has been through. When I first read that little speech about what it feels like after your kids have left the nest, I thought it was so well done, and really hit upon that emotion. It made me not want to let my kids leave!

Woody almost becomes obsessed with Forky. It's probably the case that Bonnie will be okay, so why is it so important to Woody?

I think it's twofold. We want Bonnie to be alright, and so does Woody, but it's also the deeper thing that it's a little bit of his insecurity. It's the only thing that he has got going for him, so that's going to be the thing he latches on to. Something that goes through the other films as well is that he is a very strong-willed character who is driven by fear and can get frustrated and angry, but he has blinders on to the rest of the world. So this film really is removing those blinders even more.

Another important relationship in this film is that between Woody and Bo Peep. How does that inform the story?

In pretty much every version of this film, one thing we always had was seeing the moment Bo left. It wasn't until later that I realized that it's not just seeing why she left her house, but how it affected Woody, and the choice he made there, which is, he could leave as well, but he's so dedicated to his kid that he decides not to. We have seen him confronted with that choice before, in *Toy Story 2*, where he could leave Andy and be a collector's item forever – and he was ready to do it; he was going to go to Japan. So, I don't think it's that far of a stretch to believe that he was willing to do it for Bo, as well. But that's the choice he makes at the beginning: is he going to be there for his kid, or not? How far will he go?

How would you characterize Woody's relationship with Bo this time around?

The production team went back and looked at all the scenes featuring Bo Peep in *Toy Story* and *Toy Story 2* – she only features in a couple shots in *Toy Story 3* – and besides being Woody's love interest, more importantly she's always been a character that he can speak honestly to. She gives him advice and offers a little bit of a reality check for him. There's a subtle, caring relationship there that we felt was worth tapping into for this movie – because you do wonder what happened to her: they were a thing; Woody does reference her in *Toy Story 3*, and there's obviously some pain behind that. It feels natural that we're using what we've seen and what we've heard about her, seeing how they react to each other when she's given away.

08

09

PATTY KIHM, DIRECTING ANIMATOR

How does Bo feel about being reunited with Woody after all this time?

I think she's still in love with him. At the beginning of the movie, he breaks her heart. He makes a choice to stay with the other toys. When she meets him again, she's kind of excited to see him, like an old friend, but also kind of hopes for more.

The interesting thing between these two characters is that Woody's kind of the opposite of her. She's left Andy's room and become comfortable, she enjoys life. Her world is now something much bigger, and she's at peace with it, whereas Woody's kind of nervous and he's always pining to get back to Bonnie's room. This nervous energy with this calm confident energy is really interesting to play with.

05. Woody in peril

06. Coaching Forky in the purpose of being a toy

07. Woody and Forky begin to understand each other

08. It was important for the filmmakers for Woody to have a genuine all-new character arc for this movie

09. Woody goes out of his way to guide Forky on his journey

VALERIE LAPOINTE, STORY SUPERVISOR

What does Woody get out of his relationship with Bo?

With Bo, Woody has met his match as a leader. I like to think of her as having the confidence. In the previous films we see how she's always encouraging him. She comforts him when he's having a hard time; she's the voice of reason amongst the other toys. We get to see glimpses of that in the other films.

In this film, we really get to see what the next chapter was, which was that Bo was her own leader amongst Molly's toys. When we catch up with her later, we see that she's a match for Woody, taking the next step beyond helping more toys.

How did you arrive at this new mission for Woody?

We batted around a lot of ideas for a long time on this film, and really tried to find a genuine character arc and change for Woody to go through, especially after three films. It felt natural that his next stage was transitioning from Andy to a new kid. A lot of the original people who created *Toy Story* latched onto the idea of when your kids grow up and they go to college, this next phase of the relationship changing between Woody and his kid.

In that change, and in that new part of his life, he's discovering a new sense of purpose, or a bigger purpose that he can have. It felt natural that the next step for him was to go from being there for one kid, to being there for all kids – just adding that plural sense of a bigger purpose, a bigger job he can do. ■

BO PEEP

Making a return to the *Toy Story* franchise after her appearances in the first two *Toy Story* movies, Bo Peep takes a key role in *Toy Story 4* as an unlikely action heroine!

E ver watchful of her flock: Billy, Goat, and Gruff, Bo Peep is a surprisingly sassy shepherdess with a soft spot for Woody. Smart, sensible and always ready to share her opinions, she is voiced once again by actress Annie Potts.

HENRY GARCIA, SIMULATION SUPERVISOR
Who is Bo Peep in *Toy Story 4*?
Bo Peep is our big character, and her cloak is a part of her character in the same way that Merida's hair was a part of that character in *Brave* (2012). It very much plays into her acting, how she moves, even what mode she's in. She might be in stealth mode where it's wrapped around her, hero mode where it's more like a cape, or princess mode where it's more as a skirt. Radford Hern is the digital artist who built that garment and gave it so many different variants – the inside, outside, around the shoulders and the back. Getting the cloak up and running was a big deal for the character!

Is there a version of the garment that exists in the real world?
There are two of them, actually. There's one of them in the animation department and another in the simulation department. We used them to interact to solve fairly trivial

> ## "You know, some kids play rougher than others so I try to be prepared."
> ## — Bo Peep

things. Bo has her staff, so how does that interact with her cape? Does it get caught? Does it get snagged? We would put the cape on in order to figure out how it should move on-screen!

Did you have a staff as well?
We had a staff too. It's more like a broomstick but it did the job. We simulated the body in a way that we hadn't before. On something like *The Good Dinosaur* (2015), where we had skin moving around, we do that in simulation as well. It's similar to that but in this case we used it to bring the arms to life. We're using it for subtle things that streamline our process, but you wouldn't always notice them on-screen.

01

BECKI TOWER, DIRECTING ANIMATOR

How would you describe Bo Peep's attitude to life as a toy in *Toy Story 4*?

We tried to stay away from her being an old-school fairy-tale princess where she's doe-eyed and weak, or needs someone else's validation for her own sense of value. In this movie she's very independent. She's okay with being a lost toy. She wants to live her life her way. She doesn't need to fit into the box, so to speak. She's found peace with living outside of what is normal for a toy or what their ambition should be. A lot of her character is her posture and her look. On the story end they're trying to not give everything away through dialogue.

01. Woody and Bo are finally reunited

02. Bo gets a high five from Giggle McDimples

03. Bo Peep's sheep: Billy, Goat, and Gruff

04. Bo is voiced by Annie Potts, who "brings a lot of emotion" to the character, says director Josh Cooley

05. Woody and Bo in the antiques store

06. Woody tries on Bo Peep's cape for size in this concept art

07. Concept art of Bo and her sheep

08. Concept sketches and notes for Bo and her outfit

JOSH COOLEY, DIRECTOR

What does actress Annie Potts bring to Bo?

Annie's wonderful. She brings a lot of emotion to Bo – and not just emotion: I think she completely fleshes out that character. She's heartwarming, so appealing, but also very funny and very sarcastic. She also does the same thing as Tom Hanks, where she can sell things in the room; we would workshop lines and she would come up with thoughts that would feel more natural to her. Both of them can bring a real sense of a natural performance and really thoughtful ways of bringing the character out. ■

"You would not believe the things I've seen..." – Bo Peep

07

08

stiff cape
=
simple
silhouette

when end of staff is DOWN,
it can go underneath cloak.

when end of staff is UP, it
goes in front of cloak.

Concept art: Woody and Bo's reunion

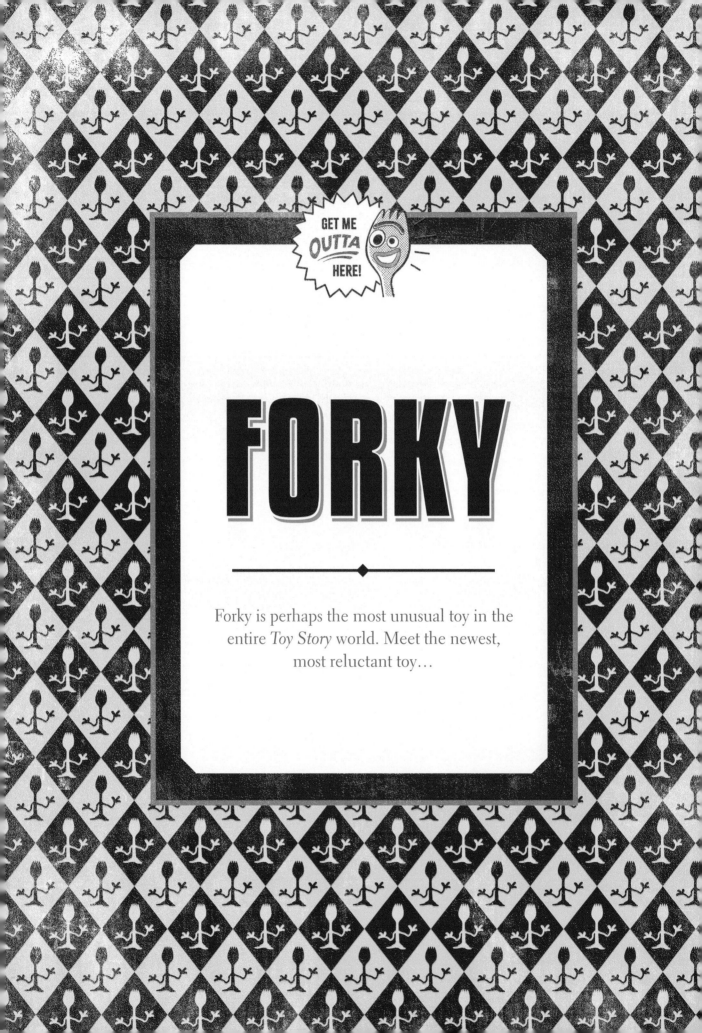

GET ME OUTTA HERE!

FORKY

Forky is perhaps the most unusual toy in the
entire *Toy Story* world. Meet the newest,
most reluctant toy…

new character joins the *Toy Story* cast: Forky, a nervous toy created from trash, finds himself under the watchful eye of Woody as they embark on an epic journey of discovery.

VALERIE LAPOINTE, STORY SUPERVISOR
What was the genesis of Forky?
When Forky first came up as an idea, we got some craft supplies in the art department, and everybody made their own version of Forky.

When Forky is created in the movie, where does he think he belongs, and why?
Basically, Forky's pieces are pulled out of the trash can. When he comes to life, we're playing with the idea that he comes alive because our central protagonist, Bonnie, made him and played with him. However, his natural instinct is to go back to what comforts him, which is being trash. He thinks of the trash as his comfort blanket that he just wants to go back to – he feels safe there, like a little kid. For Forky, that's his context of safety and home. It's where he wants to be.

Is Forky the youngster of the group of toys? Does he have a journey in understanding his role?
We're playing with the idea that he's essentially born in this moment, so he's unaware of how everything works. He doesn't know why he's alive; he doesn't know that they're toys, or what their purpose is. He's trying to figure everything out. Through the film we see this incremental progression of him learning things and figuring things out.

> ## "I don't belong here! Aaaahhhh!"
> ## – Forky

01

01. Bonnie creates her own toy, Forky, from trash and discarded art supplies

02. Valerie LaPointe: "Bonnie makes Forky, but Woody initiates it."

> # "I was made for soup, salad, maybe chili, and then the trash. I'm litter!"
> ## — Forky

What did Tony Hale's vocal performance bring to the character of Forky?

Tony is hilarious. He is such a fun, open, and personable actor to hang out with. We'd give him context of the scenario, and he would take a line and just start riffing on it. He came up with lots of one-liners and commentary for Forky that was then either used, or inspired other dialogue. He's an amazing improvisational artist, and he utilized those skills to flesh out and find the humor in Forky's character.

Is there something of a father-son relationship between Woody and Forky?

Essentially, Woody is the reason Forky is born. He is the one who throws the supplies on the table. Bonnie makes Forky, but Woody initiates it. Woody sees the moment that brings Bonnie out of her shell in class. The other toys don't witness it, so he takes it upon himself to take care of Forky. Also, it gives Woody a sense of purpose again. He has a way to help Bonnie that he's been searching for.

AXEL GEDDES, FILM EDITOR
How important is humor in *Toy Story?*

Toy Story movies are at their best when the humor comes from

06

07

the characters being in certain situations in a way that feels organic and is supporting the story. But some of the characters are inherently more funny. Forky is just an inherently funny character. Forky doesn't even have to say anything – he's funny.

Does Tony Hale, who plays Forky, give you a lot to work with?

Tony Hale is a dream to work with. He's the most open, kind, thoughtful person. I go to all the recording sessions and if anyone has an idea, he wants to hear it, and he wants to keep working a joke. It took a while to find the character because Tony had an instinct to make it really big, and we realized it's only occasionally big. Most of the time it's just subtle, quirkier, and funnier. He's a very thoughtful person and I think that comes through on that little plastic fork.

PATTY KIHM, DIRECTING ANIMATOR
What was it like working on the character of Forky?

We spent a lot of time trying to figure out Forky's arc. Because he was created in the movie, we wanted to have the audience learn with him. At first he can't really move any of his parts, and then eventually he starts to learn to use his hands, how to dart his eyes around, and actually look at things without moving his whole body. By the end of the movie he's the most articulated that we have seen him. The point is to to see him grow throughout the movie.

HENRY GARCIA, SIMULATION SUPERVISOR
What input did you have in the creation of Forky?

His arms are pipe cleaners, which in the art world is just very stiff hair. We didn't simulate it much at all, but there are a few occasions where we did. There are a couple of scenes where a character might squeeze his arm, and you actually see the hair on the pipe cleaner deform away. The second thing we set up on Forky was built for the animation department. When he's in toy mode, when he's not alive but is just being played with, he has googly eyes that swim around, so we set up the physics-based simulator to make those eyes move. The simulator then breaks that down into data that animation can tweak and adjust and move and finesse if they want. ∎

SPACE RANGER
ACTION FIGURE

BUZZ LIGHTYEAR

Tim Allen looks back at the long-standing
success of *Toy Story*, his involvement from
the very beginning and how he had a hand
in changing the course of its destiny.

A toy space ranger, Buzz Lightyear has been a key part in the *Toy Story* franchise since he joined Woody and the gang in Andy's room back in 1995. Voiced, as ever, by Tim Allen, *Toy Story 4* sees Buzz join the toys on their most epic adventure yet.

Toy Story 4: The Official Movie Special: When you were first approached, in the early 1990s, about supplying your voice to a character in a totally computer-animated film, what was your reaction?

Tim Allen: "What!?" (Laughs) Actually, I'm kind of a computer geek, so it didn't scare me as much as the fact I'd never done voice work before. It was key personnel that sold it to me – they've all got such passion. "It'll be fun, and your character will be this. And it's got toys coming to life."

What was your original take on the character of Buzz Lightyear?

They asked me how I would do the character, and initially Buzz started as this big, brassy disc jockey voice, then I pulled it back a bit.

What did you think about the concept of the movie?

What a cool idea! Toys come to life. I didn't know it would be hours in a studio alone with a director. "Uh-huh. I don't like it. Start from the top, please." And there are no other actors. I like audiences or something, rather than, "Uh-huh." You're working all alone in a room. It's not very sexy, how animated movies are done. However, the pleasant part is seeing the finished film on-screen, and how they fold what you've done into the movie. *Toy Story* was spectacular and *Toy Story 2* built on the original, and so on. No matter where you get into it, it's mesmerizing.

How would you describe Buzz Lightyear to someone who hasn't seen the films?

Buzz Lightyear is the newest toy in the toy box. He has to introduce himself to the other toys. Toys only speak when people aren't looking. As soon as you walk away, all of your toys know each other and talk. And Buzz Lightyear has to go through the process of learning that he's not his persona, which is an action figure on a cartoon. He is just one of the action figures that people bought, but he thinks he's the real guy on TV. The process of *Toy Story* is figuring out that he's not. Then in the subsequent movies, the process is that it doesn't matter. He's still that guy. He becomes authentic even though he's not the real deal.

"This planet is toxic.
Prepare to hyper-sleep!"
— Buzz Lightyear

01. The friends are reunited!

02. Buzz flanked by Jessie and Dolly

03. Faced with another crisis, Rex asks, "What would Woody do?" Buzz's response: "Jump out of a moving vehicle?"

03

What about some of the other toys?

Well, all the girls really like him. Once the girls get around Buzz, they go for him, even though he's got a little bit of a Napoleon complex. He's a little small. I originally thought, "Guys, you couldn't have made him less intimidating?" But Buzz could kick Woody's butt at any point. He just won't. The best relationship is with [Woody's voice actor Tom] Hanks, both personally and on-screen. It's a classic buddy relationship.

Are there any similarities between you and Buzz?

Honestly, no. This is a character that I got to create completely, working with the team at Pixar. It was an open book. What would Buzz be like? And I got to present this character. But he's a somewhat deluded guy, who sometimes doesn't speak very well and misses words. Well, I guess there is one thing. I somewhat live in my own world, you know, like Buzz. "Are you still there?" I still have that delusion. And I expand on it. I'm a comedian, so I'm able to get away with exaggeration as reality.

When the concept of a fully computer-generated film came along, did you have any idea that the finished film would look the way it does?

I knew exactly what Pixar was before they did the original *Toy Story*, because I loved digital animation in college. I had seen this piece about a lamp chasing a ball around. But actually, as

a feature, I had no idea. I thought it was startling. I sat down and watched it with some Disney execs and cel animators, and even they thought it was startling. As a film buff, what is amazing about these animated movies is the light source. I love lighting. It's a big part of all filmmaking. But in digital, you can set the light source and move it around as though the day is going quicker. If you know about movies, the light source can come from any direction and all directions at the same time – the sun or a light that's come on. But look at an animated movie sometime – they can manipulate as though the sun's coming from all different angles. It's a very subtle thing, but it's amazing to watch. The first thing I noticed in the first *Toy Story* was, "Where is the light source coming from?" They can change it in the middle of a scene. It can move. I didn't know if they were doing it consciously. It's the huge difference between live action and digital films.

Is it true that you encouraged Disney to release the first *Toy Story* in theaters?

There was some consideration of the film being released in theaters or possibly just on VHS cassette at the time. I said, "No, this is a big movie." I thought it would be great for Disney. There was a great relationship between the two main characters. Even the sequel was the same. They thought they should do the sequel for video. I said, "No, these are movies. This is big stuff for you guys."

> "The slingshot maneuver is all we've got. Full speed ahead!"
> – Buzz Lightyear

JOSH COOLEY, DIRECTOR
What's Buzz's story in this film?

Buzz has to see that Woody makes a change. Early on in the film, he's trying to be very supportive for Woody, and helping him out. He gives Woody the advice that Woody gave him early on: to listen to your inner voice. We played it for a gag most of the movie with Buzz, but at the end it's played with emotion. ■

DUCKY & BUNNY

A pair of carnival prizes, Ducky and Bunny
may be polar opposites but they share a
special connection, and are both desperate to
find a loving home…

Quite literally inseparable, Ducky and Bunny are carnival prizes desperate to be won by a child. Voiced by Keegan-Michael Key and Jordan Peele, they are *Toy Story*'s latest double act, striving to find love.

VALERIE LAPOINTE, STORY SUPERVISOR

What can you tell us about Ducky and Bunny?

Early on in production, the idea came up of having a carnival in the film. It felt like a location we had never explored in any of the *Toy Story* films, or short films, and it's obviously a natural place for toys to live. Ducky and Bunny came into existence early on in the process as paired toys. The idea is that carnival toys are stuck there because they are rarely won, because the games are so hard or they're rigged. Ducky and Bunny have been hanging out in the carnival for so many years and desperately want to be won by a kid.

They have the same aspiration as Gabby Gabby, who wants that experience of being owned by a kid. However, Ducky and Bunny have a misperception of what that means, and how the world works, because they've only seen it from their limited viewpoint.

How much did Keegan-Michael Key and Jordan Peele bring to the characters?

Keegan and Jordan doing their voices brought so much to Ducky and Bunny's personalities. We had something written, and they were just riffing on that; it was amazing to watch them bring those characters to life. They really add a lot of humor to the film.

01. "Literally inseparable" Ducky and Bunny join the gang

02. Buzz and Giggle McDimples, flanked by Ducky and Bunny, hatch a plan

03. The team spy the sought-after key

"If you think you can just show up here and take our top prize spot, you're wrong. DEAD WRONG." — Ducky and Bunny

04. Buzz becomes the latest carnival prize

05. *Toy Story*'s newest toys encounter some friendly faces

06. Concept sketches of Ducky and Bunny

PATTY KIHM: DIRECTING ANIMATOR

How would you describe Ducky and Bunny?

Ducky and Bunny are attached at the hand, but Ducky has this frenetic energy; he's like a bouncing ball who can't stop. He's attached to Bunny who's heavier so he can't move as fast as this little ball of energy.

What's it like to animate two plush characters?

Ducky could have gone a number of ways, but we ended up treating his mouth kind of like Kermit the Frog's. Ducky can pull his beak in and open and close it, but that wasn't enough. To be more expressive, it gave us more range to treat it more like a handheld puppet.

Bunny's mouth is very limited. It's this tiny little bucktooth mouth. He is half-lidded and slower, and it's not just because of his sheer size. He's a heavier character, and he's not as quick as Ducky in terms of figuring things out! ■

"I don't care which cabbage patch you're from, kid, give me back my Viewmaster before I knock the dimples off your face!"
— Bunny

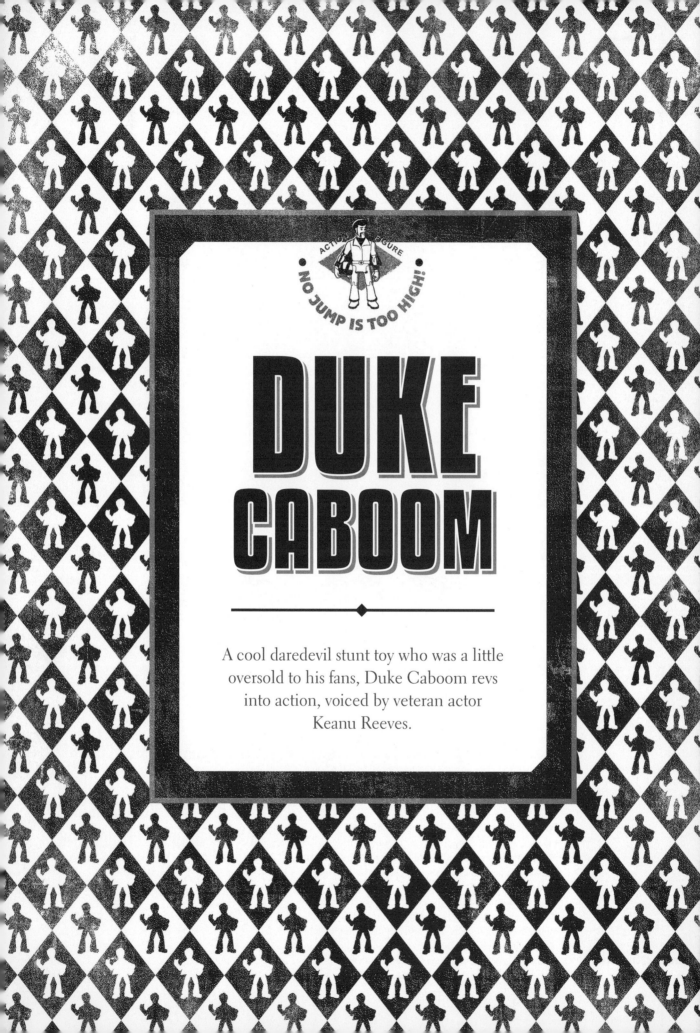

ACTION FIGURE

NO JUMP IS TOO HIGH!

DUKE CABOOM

A cool daredevil stunt toy who was a little
oversold to his fans, Duke Caboom revs
into action, voiced by veteran actor
Keanu Reeves.

A daredevil on two wheels, Duke Caboom is an action toy, ready to race into danger at a moment's notice. However, despite his brash boasts, he isn't quite as cool as he seems, despite being voiced by Hollywood superstar, Keanu Reeves.

JOSH COOLEY, DIRECTOR
Who is Duke Caboom?

Duke Caboom is a 1970s toy that wasn't quite as good as the commercial said he was, and that's something that's been eating away at him for years. One kid that owned him discarded him because he couldn't perform as well as the commercial said he could, so that's in this character's weak spot: he's this bombastic stuntman, but then once you bring up his kid, he crumbles to pieces.

We knew that Duke Caboom would be a Canadian stuntman, so we were thinking about Canadian actors, and Keanu was mentioned. That already made me laugh. When we met with him to talk about the character, he brought so many great questions to the table that I was not prepared for: "What's driving this guy? What's his past?" I was thinking, *Whoa, okay…!* I just thought this was a side joke character, but I realized I really needed to think about this. I talked to Keanu over the phone a couple times, about how Duke's not mad at the kid who owned him; he's mad at himself because he couldn't live up to the expectation, and he's mad at the toy manufacturer that put him in this position, and it's still eating away at him. It was great to see Keanu really trying to understand this character and what's driving him.

> "Duke's mad at himself because he couldn't live up to the expectation."
> — Josh Cooley, Director

04

01. Canadian daredevil on two wheels Duke Caboom with Giggle McDimples

02 & 03.
Concept art and final shot for the scene from Duke's past depicting his Boxing Day performance...

04. Concept sketch of Duke Caboom

AXEL GEDDES, FILM EDITOR

What was Keanu Reeves like to work with?

He's perfectly cast for the part. He's a thoughtful person and he just fit right in. I think it really surprised us that he was even an option, because it seems like he's such a big star! Keanu's also inherently funny and in some way we're channeling his Bill and Ted, while also leveraging his action hero status. He has good comic timing.

What sort of things did Keanu bring to the role?

One of the things he brought to us was an idea that I think we're just touching on. I wish we were doing a little bit more of it! We don't explain it, it's as though it's always been there, the idea that Duke is always posing. He has all these crazy poses – that was all Keanu's idea. He said, "What if he saw the box and saw all the poses that Duke did, what if he was just practicing those all the time?" I think that's when he jumped up on the table in the atrium to show an example of what that would be. [*Laughs*] Keanu is very dedicated to his work!

VALERIE LAPOINTE, STORY SUPERVISOR

What about Duke Caboom? What can you reveal about him?

Duke Caboom is a little action figure from the 1970s, Canada's greatest stuntman. Duke Caboom was immediately

> **"Duke has all these crazy poses –
> that was all Keanu Reeves' idea!"
> – Axel Geddes, Film Editor**

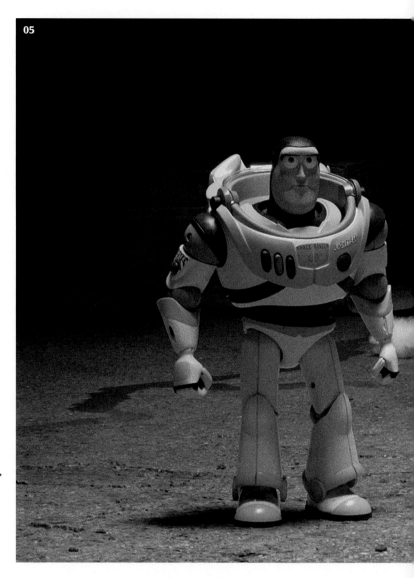

05

06

rejected by his kid as soon as he was opened because he couldn't make the jump. It's been this painful psychological issue he's been dealing with ever since then, that he can't get over, and he has zero confidence because of how he was rejected. It also gives us a chance to see how Bo Peep is amazing at giving other toys confidence and motivating them to move forward.

NEIL HELM, CROWDS LEAD
How did you approach the scene where we first meet Duke Caboom? What kind of direction did you give the animators for this sequences?

The basic story of this scene is Woody and Bo navigating their way through this big crowd of antique toys, and then at the end they meet Duke Caboom. Right behind Duke there was a group of toys sitting there, placed back there by the layout department. We took that whole second half of the sequence, and we gave all of those background toys to our

crowds animators and said, "Just have fun. Come up with a storyline for what's happening with those toys, because we're going to keep cutting back and forth between Woody and Bo and Duke, and you're always going to see that same group of toys back there behind Duke."

So the animators just had fun. They came up with this whole backstory for Luchador: he just broke up with his girlfriend, he's upset, he's had a little too much to drink, he falls asleep, and then he hugs one of his friends… They came up with this amazing story, and then we had it happening back there as this little Easter Egg bit people get to discover. Everyone loved it, but it was a little too distracting. We're supposed to be looking at Duke Caboom, and we're thinking, "What's going on with Luchador? That's kind of interesting." It was great, and the director, Josh [Cooley], loved it, but we had to pull it. The odyssey of Luchador is still there, but you can barely see it in the final movie. You can't distract from the main action. ∎

05. Duke Caboom knew Bo Peep previously and helped her find her sheep

06. "It was great to see Keanu [Reeves] really trying to understand this character." – Josh Cooley, Director

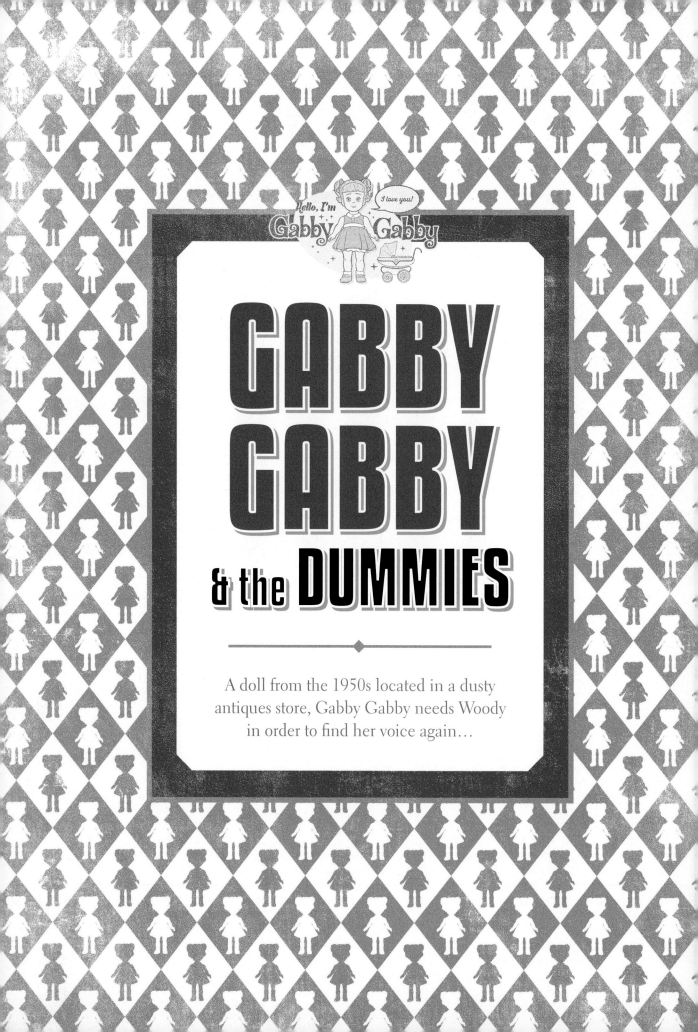

GABBY GABBY

& the DUMMIES

A doll from the 1950s located in a dusty antiques store, Gabby Gabby needs Woody in order to find her voice again…

Voiced by Christina Hendricks, Gabby Gabby is a vintage talking doll with a broken voice box. Bitter and resentful from a life as an unwanted toy in the Second Chance antiques store and armed with her ventriloquist dummy henchmen, *Toy Story 4*'s new antagonist has her eye on taking Woody's voice box for herself...

JOSH COOLEY, DIRECTOR
Can you tell us a bit about Gabby Gabby?
When Woody is looking for Bo he bumps into Gabby Gabby. She's a talking doll from the 1950s and she's been in the antiques store for a long time. She's broken so she does not have a working voice box. Woody is more interested in looking for Bo, but Gabby Gabby is very interested in the fact that Woody has a working voice box so that she can fix herself.

They decide that they were created at about the same time, probably in the same factory by the same toy company. So, their pieces are probably compatible.

Was Gabby Gabby always intended to be a creepy doll with a mysterious side?
Yes. We had to try to figure out how creepy she should be right from the get-go. Early on, I didn't want her to be a nice, friendly character, who then, all of a sudden, turns on our heroes. So, I purposefully made her the opposite, which was I wanted her to be evil right from the start. It's easy to do when she's a creepy doll walking around in the dark with ventriloquist dummies.

The audience can see that there is a mystery about her right away. So, they are thinking, "Oh, I don't like this. Woody needs to get out of there."

01. Gabby Gabby and Benson pull Woody's pull string

02, 03, & 04. Concept art for Gabby Gabby

01

Why is the antiques shop such a cool setting for this story?

We've never been in an antiques store before. We've seen toy stores, we've seen day cares, and various other locations. This is a new location and there's always tons of toys in antiques stores. My parents are big antiques collectors, so growing up that was always a thing and I've been to a lot of those stores.

There's something very interesting about going back in time, and about briefly visiting the past. Usually antiques stores are based on nostalgia, so you see things that you used to have and think, "Oh, man I wish I had that again." That's kind of how Woody is with Bo, he wishes that he still had that relationship with her.

The antiques store is a place that takes Woody back in time or like he's going back in time, just from a toy point of view. It just felt really cool. To have a bunch of toys that we've never seen before that aren't new and aren't shiny and being played with, that are rusty and wooden, and are different types of toys that helped to expand the world.

PATTI KIHM, DIRECTING ANIMATOR
Who are the dummies?

There's Benson, the main dummy, and then he has three henchmen. They're really creepy, in a good way. At first we were playing them stiff and upright, but then one of the animators brought in a version where his head was completely knocked over to the side and he has no limbs. The way he walks is like his arms and ankles are broken, and he has no control. There's a scene where they're chasing Woody and Forky through the antiques mall, and it's so scary. Kids are going to be terrified! But those characters are there to support Gabby Gabby. ◼

PET PATROL IS *Always* ON DUTY

GIGGLE McDIMPLES

A close confidante of Bo Peep, Officer Giggle McDimples may be tiny but she's got a big heart.

Ally Maki voices the tiniest addition to the *Toy Story 4* gang: Pet Patrol Officer Giggle McDimples. Although miniature in stature, she is larger than life in personality and can frequently be found on Bo Peep's shoulder dishing out the brutally honest advice that only a best friend can give.

JOSH COOLEY, DIRECTOR
Who is Giggle McDimples?
Giggle McDimples is probably the smallest toy we've done in the *Toy Story* world. She's a 1980s toy that Bo Peep finds in an antiques store and they became best friends. She's always hanging out on Bo's shoulder, almost like Jiminy Cricket or a devil and angel on Bo's shoulder giving you advice. She's a character that can speak Bo's mind without having to hear it directly from Bo.

VALERIE LAPOINTE, STORY SUPERVISOR
What is Giggle's relationship to Bo?
Giggle is Bo's best friend. Giggle is a tiny character who lives in her own little compact. Pet patrol officer is her toy title job – she has her little compact, that's her police station with her little car inside. She travels around with Bo, and they go for playtime wherever they can get it – playgrounds, anywhere. We think of her as Bo's confidante. We imply that they've been together for years, all through their time at the store – probably before the store – so they know pretty much everything about each other. They're living this lost toy life together. ∎

> ## "They're living this lost toy life together." – Valerie LaPointe, Story Supervisor

01. Pet Patrol Officer Giggle McDimples lays down the law from her compact home

02. Giggle is often found on the shoulder of her best friend, Bo

DOLLY

Introduced as the "evil witch" of Bonnie's imagination in *Toy Story 3*, Dolly makes a return as the leader of the toys in Bonnie's room...

t's time for Woody to step aside as Dolly, voiced by Bonnie Hunt, continues her job as Chief of Bonnie's ragtag gang of toys.

JOSH COOLEY, DIRECTOR
Who is the leader of Bonnie's toys?
Dolly is the leader of the room – the leader of Bonnie's toys. We showed that in *Toy Story 3*, so there was no reason to undo that. It felt like that's naturally what it is right now, and we should continue that so that Woody doesn't have that role that he used to have. ■

> "Woody? Really? You're gonna stick with that? 'Cause now's your time to change it. That's coming from a doll named Dolly." – Dolly, *Toy Story 3*

01. Dolly looks on anxiously as the toys receive some bad news

02. Dolly and her fellow toys

SUPPORTING TOYS

A *Toy Story* movie wouldn't be the same
without the key supporting characters,
and *Toy Story 4* sees the welcome
return of some old friends...

JESSIE
Voiced by: Joan Cusack
First Appearance: *Toy Story 2* (1999)
Also appears in:
Toy Story 3
Toy Story 4
Toy Story Toons
Toy Story OF TERROR!
Toy Story That Time Forgot

SLINKY DOG
Voiced by: Jim Varney (*Toy Story, Toy Story 2*),
Blake Clark (*Toy Story 3, Toy Story 4*)
First Appearance: *Toy Story* (1995)
Also appears in:
Toy Story 2
Toy Story 3
Toy Story 4
Toy Story Toons

HAMM

Voiced by: John Ratzenberger
First appearance: *Toy Story* (1995)
Also appears in:
Toy Story 2
Toy Story 3
Toy Story 4
Toy Story Treats
Toy Story Toons

> "We're next month's garage sale fodder for sure."
> – Hamm panics at the arrival of new toys, *Toy Story*

PEAS-IN-A-POD

Voiced by: Charlie Bright (Peatey)
Amber Kroner (Peatrice)
Brianna Maiwand (Peanelope)
First Appearance: *Toy Story 3* (2010)
Also appear in:
Toy Story 3
Toy Story 4
Toy Story Toons

MR. AND MRS. POTATO HEAD

Voiced by: Don Rickles and Estelle Harris
First appearance (Mr. Potato Head): *Toy Story* (1995)
First appearance (Mrs. Potato Head): *Toy Story 2* (1999)
Also appear in:
Toy Story 2
Toy Story 3
Toy Story 4
Toy Story Toons
Toy Story OF TERROR!
Toy Story That Time Forgot

"The Potato Heads, Mr. and Mrs. You've gotta keep 'em together 'cause they're madly in love."

– Andy explains Mr. and Mrs. Potato Head's relationship to Bonnie, *Toy Story 3*

"This is Rex! The meanest, most terrifying dinosaur who ever lived!"
– Andy introduces Rex to Bonnie, *Toy Story 3*

REX

Voiced by: Wallace Shawn
First appearance: *Toy Story* (1995)
Also appears in:
Toy Story 2
Toy Story 3
Toy Story 4
Toy Story Toons
Toy Story OF TERROR!
Toy Story That Time Forgot
Toy Story Treats

COMBAT CARL JR.

Voiced by: Carl Weathers
First appearance: *Toy Story* (1995)
Also appears in:
Toy Story 4
Toy Story Treats
Toy Story OF TERROR!

BUTTERCUP
Voiced by: Jeff Garlin
First appearance: *Toy Story 3* (2010)
Also appears in:
Toy Story 4
Toy Story Toons

MR. PRICKLEPANTS
Voiced by: Timothy Dalton
First appearance: *Toy Story 3* (2010)
Also appears in:
Toy Story 4
Toy Story Toons
Toy Story OF TERROR!
Toy Story That Time Forgot

THE ALIENS

Voiced by: Jeff Pidgeon
First appearance: *Toy Story* (1995)
Also appear in:
Toy Story 2
Toy Story 3
Toy Story 4
Toy Story Treats
Toy Story Toons

TRIXIE

Voiced by: Kristen Schaal
First appearance: *Toy Story 3* (2010)
Also appears in:
Toy Story 4
Toy Story Toons
Toy Story OF TERROR!
Toy Story That Time Forgot

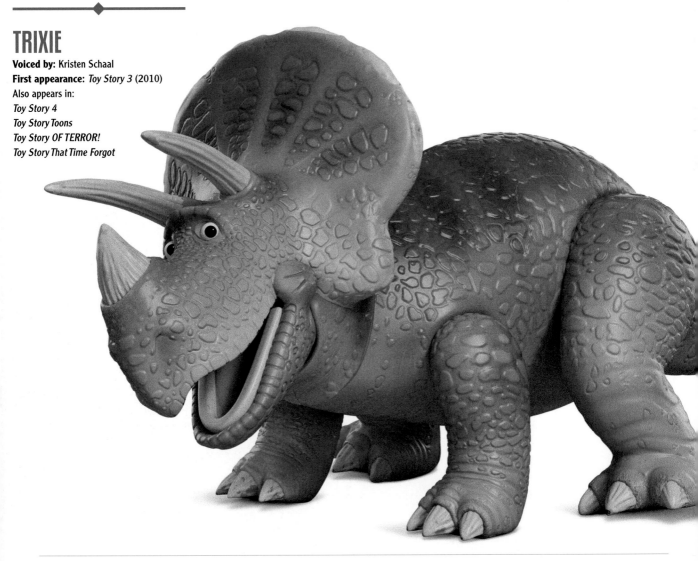

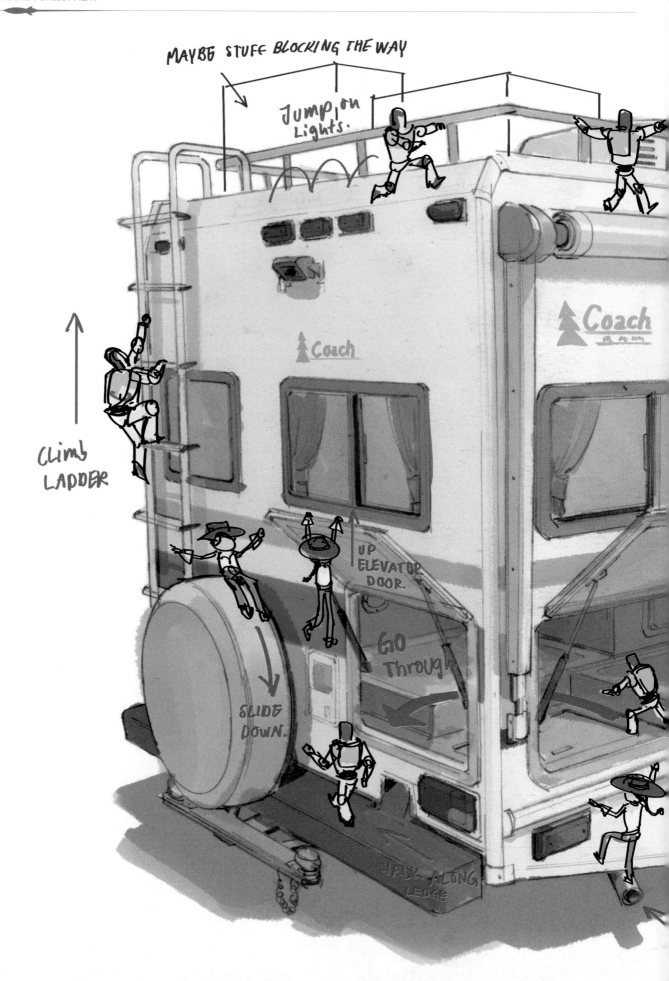

WALK ALONG AWNING.

RUN
along
Ledge.

land
on exhaust pipe

Concept art: Detail of the RV

ANIMATED DISCUSSIONS

Woody, Buzz, and the rest of the *Toy Story* cast depend on the talented team behind the scenes to make their adventures come alive...

THE SETS OF *TOY STORY 4*

One of the major challenges of designing sets for *Toy Story 4* was anticipating the multitude of angles that would be used during filming.

DANIEL HOLLAND, SET DESIGNER

Are there rules to the world of *Toy Story*, in terms of the look?

The world is the real world. Had they had the technology when they made the first *Toy Story*, it would have been more realistic. So, we lean toward realism, as opposed to more of a super-designed mode. If we're in an antiques mall, it needs to be a place that feels like it's a building in a town that's had a history. That's the kind of thing I'm trying to do: create a sense of realism, so you believe this place existed before this film was made.

Can you tell us about the design aesthetic behind some of the locations in the film?

We start out in Bonnie's house, her bedroom. We designed the whole house to actually make sense, but we only really see her bedroom. I guess one way to describe the designs of this world is, it's Anytown, USA. It's the Midwest-ish, but it's also supposed to be something that everyone can relate to. Bonnie's school reflects that kind of feel: built in the '50s, and then updated a little bit in the late '60s.

Then we go on a road trip, moving in one day from Ohio all the way over to Cody, Wyoming. So we looked at Cody, Wyoming as a place to draw inspiration from. It's a mountain, western kind of town. There's a carnival coming through town – the kind that everyone sees everywhere – and

there's the antiques mall, which is the place I was talking about before. I think originally it was a furniture store from the late '30s, early '40s; it's had 10 different owners over its life, and things have been torn out and rearranged. So you see a little bit of what was originally there, but you also see some stuff that was done badly in the '70s, like some drywall that was slapped up, and a couple of walls taken out here and there. On Gabby Gabby's cabinet, you can see where it used to have some letters that said "cosmetics" – that was a built-in cosmetics counter. It's giving the film a sense of a place you've seen before, because you've been in hundreds of these places, these buildings that have histories. That was what we were trying to do.

Let's talk about the carnival. Did you have to become experts on building Ferris wheels, and the rides, and that type of thing?

Visually, you do have to become an expert in how things would be built and look, and what makes sense. That's something that I do love about working in sets: I love building things. I love thinking about how things are produced. I look at these chairs and think, "How were they put together? Where are the welt joints that make sense? Why do they have screws the way they do? What's holding this on…?" So that is in my favor when trying to design and build architecture and rides and things like that.

01. Two of *Toy Story 4*'s stars, Bo Peep and Giggle McDimples

02. Concept sketch of Bonnie's classroom

03. Concept sketch of the pinball machine hideout, Tinny's

04. Painted concept art of the carnival

05. Concept painting of the antiques store

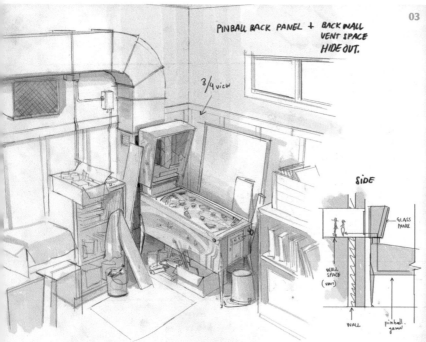

THE ANIMATION OF *TOY STORY 4*

Having worked at Pixar for over 20 years, Patty Kihm has gained plenty of experience that was put to good use as a Directing Animator on *Toy Story 4*.

PATTY KIHM, DIRECTING ANIMATOR

What's the difference between a directing animator and a supervising animator?

Supervising animators have to go to all the meetings I don't want to go to! They oversee all of the animation production; they're the liaison between animation and production. We're on the floor going to each animator's offices and solving problems. If they have questions, we're their point person.

Are there certain characters that you've taken to while working on *Toy Story 4*?

I started working on this movie in early 2018. Other directing animators have been on much, much longer, but when I came on, I kind of adopted Bo as my character, and helped model her and put together models for all the animators to look at. Usually when Bo Peep shots come up, they ask my opinion. So, Bo Peep is my character, really.

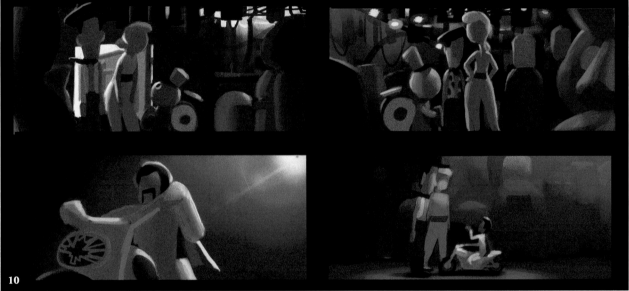

THE PHYSICS OF *TOY STORY 4*

Henry Garcia and his team were charged with creating things so real you'll forget they were made with a computer...

HENRY GARCIA, SIMULATION SUPERVISOR
What is the role of a Simulation Supervisor?
We use physics in order to make things move, as opposed to animation that moves things by hand. We use computers but we apply physics onto clothing, hair, grass, rope, trees and all those kinds of things to bring them to life.

What other elements have you worked on that people should watch out for?
This is a little personal to me, so perhaps slightly selfish. My son is hard of hearing and wears a cochlear implant; an oversized hearing aid with a piece on top. When Mara,

who's in the characters department, was doing an overall diversity pass on the classroom sequence, one of the things we did was put a kid there wearing a hearing device – we had to interact with the hair and get it placed perfectly.

Does your son know that he has been represented in the movie?
He does. He's eight and actually looks a lot like the kid that's in there too, which is awesome. He likes to think he's famous! It wasn't a big task for us by any means. Let's go a little bit extra here to make sure that we build a world that's true to the one we live in and all of its diversity that we have.

06. Bo Peep, Patty Kihm's favorite character

07. Concept art of a Bo and Woody scene

08. The day-care sequence holds a special place in Henry Garcia's heart

09. Concept art showing Woody approaching the antiques store

10. Storyboards for a scene with Bo, Woody, and Duke Caboom

THE EDITING OF *TOY STORY 4*

Consider Axel Geddes an authority on the life of toys, having worked on three *Toy Story* movies as well as three shorts based on the franchise.

AXEL GEDDES, FILM EDITOR

What's your relationship to the world of *Toy Story*?

I've been working on *Toy Story 4* for a little over two years, since finishing on *Finding Dory*. I worked on *Toy Story 2* and *Toy Story 3*, and the shorts *Partysaurus Rex*, *Hawaiian Vacation*, and *Toy Story OF TERROR!*

Having worked on so many *Toy Story* productions, did the new film present any challenges?

We spent a lot of time trying to find its voice, trying to differentiate from the first three films while also feeling like it's part of the canon. There are numerous characters in every *Toy Story* film, so we were trying to find where each character naturally fit and how their voice could be heard while also continuing to keep track of Woody's story. Every *Toy Story* film is like a juggling act of other characters so that they are servicing the main character. That's one of the biggest struggles of every *Toy Story* project I've been on. We want to feel like we've spent time with all the gang, and the gang gets bigger.

What is it about the previous films that make them so special?

There's a universe to this story, for anyone that was fortunate enough to have a toy, or many toys. Even if you don't have a toy I'm assuming you probably create toys, things that are around you so that you breathe life into them. What makes *Toy Story* special is that it's making them a real thing; it just feels like something we're all familiar with. In a way, it feels like home to a lot of people who have grown up with the movies. You don't want to disappoint them – you want this movie to feel like new territory, but also feel like home.

How does director Josh Cooley work within the editing room?

Josh is very open to collaboration. He reacts well to things that he's seen. I think some people can hear the pitch and see it. He's more of a director who feels it. When we can spend the time in edit we can craft the scenes in a great way. We can get the gags right. Josh is very, very funny. He really has a deep understanding of the oddball humor. ∎

11

12

13

14

THE MUSIC OF *TOY STORY 4*

A key element in the *Toy Story* world is the music
by Randy Newman, who returns to score *Toy Story 4*.

JOSH COOLEY, DIRECTOR

How did the collaboration with Randy Newman work on *Toy Story 4*?

Randy is just like Tom Hanks. He knows this world so well. Randy's music defines these movies and I couldn't imagine making a fourth one without him. His music is the language of this film. I can recall driving with my kids in the back of the car watching *Toy Story*, and just hearing the music. I could see the movie in my head just by listening to Woody run across a room. Everything I could hear was telling me that the kids were watching *Toy Story*.

It was essential that Randy was involved with this film. I just let him do his thing. I knew that he'd bring it, so I just had to make sure that the music was following the story. The collaboration part of it is really to just let him be amazing.

What is the difference between this score and his previous *Toy Story* music?

One thing that was important to me was that "You've Got a Friend in Me" – whether it's the song, or whether it's that melody woven into the score – represented Andy, and Woody's time with Andy. I wanted to be conscious of that

and not make it feel similar to the other films in that sense. It was only when we were referencing Andy, or show him on-screen, that we actually used that theme. We wanted Bonnie's theme to be something completely different.

One thing I did ask for was for there to be echoes of the first *Toy Story* in the theme with Bo and Woody together, so it reminds us of their relationship from the other films as well. Bo has a theme in there that is similar to what we've heard with her before.

11. *Toy Story 4* –
the story of Woody...
and friends

12. Woody and Forky
hanging out!

13. Concept portrait of
Bonnie and her family

14. Concept sketch of a
Woody and Forky scene

15. Bonnie latches
onto her new best
friend, Forky!

15

Concept art: Woody and Duke
Caboom head to the carnival

HEY HOWDY HEY

OPENING THE TOY BOX

Before the *Toy Story* franchise became a global phenomenon, a small animation company had to rewrite the rules of cinema.

01. *Toy Story*'s main protaginists, Buzz Lightyear and Woody

02. Jessie, a foil for Woody who made her debut in *Toy Story 2*

03. Slinky Dog, a wooden toy dachshund who speaks with a distinctive Southern accent

01

PIXAR BEGINS

Pixar was founded in 1979 as the Computer Division of Lucasfilm, Ltd. George Lucas recruited Dr. Ed Catmull, then director of the Computer Graphics Laboratory at the New York Institute of Technology, to develop state-of-the-art computer technology for the film industry. Dr. Catmull's group – which included video graphics designer Ralph Guggenheim, animator William Reeves and director/animator John Lasseter – went on to produce computer animation sequences for *Star Trek II: The Wrath of Khan* (1982), *Star Wars: Return of the Jedi* (1983), and *Young Sherlock Holmes* (1985). In 1986, Steve Jobs acquired Pixar and it was registered as an independent company.

Pixar's relationship with The Walt Disney Company dates back to 1989, when the two companies embarked on a joint technical development effort that resulted in CAPS (Computer Animated Production System), the Academy Award®-winning 2D computer animation production system. Disney first experimented with CAPS for a scene in *The Little Mermaid* (1991) and has gone on to use the system for all of its subsequent animated features. Expanding upon their creative partnership on CAPS, Disney and Pixar entered into a three-picture production deal in 1991 with *Toy Story* being green-lit first.

A number of Pixar's rendering software products have become commercially available and are now the industry standard. The best known is RenderMan, which is the Academy Award®-winning computer technology used by motion picture and television studios to create realistic special effects.

Inspired by the 1988 Pixar short, *Tin Toy*, *Toy Story* represents a major milestone in animated moviemaking with its groundbreaking graphic style adding to the believability of a world where toys have a life of their own. With the screenplay including material by Joss Whedon and Andrew Stanton, a cast of top vocal talent headed by Tom Hanks and Tim Allen, plus three new songs and an inspired score by renowned composer/performer Randy Newman, the fantasy takes flight.

Just as Disney's experimental shorts of the 1930s served as a proving ground for that Studio's first feature, *Snow White and the Seven Dwarfs* (1937), so too did Pixar experiment with a series of award-winning shorts to prepare them for their feature film debut. By way of comparison, *Jurassic Park*, which used computer graphics to create several of its impressive dinosaur sequences, had six minutes of CGI (computer generated imagery) and *Casper* (1995) has 40 minutes compared to the 77 minutes (or 1,561 shots) produced by Pixar for *Toy Story*.

> ◆ Pixar has been responsible for almost every major breakthrough in the application of computer graphics to filmmaking. ◆

THE TOYS COME OUT TO PLAY

Set in a world where toys have a life of their own when people are not present, *Toy Story* features the voices of two-time Academy Award®-winning actor Tom Hanks, popular television comic Tim Allen and a wonderful cast of acting talents. The story focuses on the relationship between two rival toys. There's Woody (Tom Hanks), a traditional pull-string talking cowboy, who has long enjoyed a place of honor as the favorite among six-year-old Andy's menagerie of toys. Admired and respected by the other toys, he is the de facto leader who keeps the peace between the various and disparate personalities who tend to bicker amongst themselves. Quick to calm their anxieties about being replaced by newer arrivals, Woody finds his own confidence shaken and his status as top toy in jeopardy with the arrival of Buzz Lightyear (Tim Allen), the coolest space action figure ever made.

02

03

04

To help get Tom Hanks enthused about the role, an animation test was created, using Hanks' voice from the *Turner & Hooch* soundtrack.

THE STORY

For several months in 1991, the Pixar story team held brainstorming sessions in a tiny room code-named "The Point" at the far end of the Tech building in Point Richmond, California. With no phones and a blank canvas, the team delved into their childhood, sketching ideas and scenarios that would amount to more than 25,000 storyboards.

"Everybody is an authority on their childhood and their toys. On that level this was an easy film to write," relates co-writer Andrew Stanton. "The way we work in the creation process is we completely ignore the medium we are writing for because it handcuffs us. Any technological achievements we've made in this medium came after we already committed to the storyline."

To help get Tom Hanks enthused about the role, an animation test with Woody was created, using Hanks' voice from the *Turner & Hooch* soundtrack. The dialogue for the test lasted only four seconds – long enough to win the actor's approval. Hanks recalls, "The dialogue was 'Not the

car. Don't eat the car! Not the car!' and Woody was just flailing in hysterics. He dropped to his knees and his little fists pounded the ground. It was really amazing."

Hanks' comic gifts brought an added dimension to the character, especially when it came to expressing Woody's uniquely sarcastic personality. "On the surface, Woody is very loose, very relaxed about everything. He sees himself as Mr. Nice Guy. But underneath he's thinking, who's my competition and what do I have to do to stay on top?" explains *Toy Story*'s supervising animator Pete Docter.

Defining the persona of Buzz Lightyear proved more difficult, although Buzz's personality blossomed once Tim Allen was cast. First, envisioning Buzz as a Dudley Do-Right kind of super hero, after the first recording session with Allen their perspective shifted. Instead of making Buzz aware of being a super hero, Pixar made him more like a well-trained cop.

For the supporting characters, the team decided to use existing toys, mixed in with those invented for the film. It gave the story a reality and sense of nostalgia. A prerequisite for the inclusion of existing toys was that they stood the test of time. "We didn't want to look back in 10 years and see that nobody knew what those toys were," says Stanton. "So we used only the classics, like Mr. Potato Head, Slinky Dog, Etch A Sketch, Green Army Men, Magic 8 Ball, and Barrel of Monkeys."

On the urging of Disney, the writers worked hard to give their story an edge, rather than making it seem juvenile. Consequently, when toys came alive they acted like adults doing their jobs. Andy's room was their workplace, and when Andy wasn't around a set of rules existed.

04. Mr. and Mrs. Potato Head, two characters based on existing toys

05. Mr Pricklepants, Buttercup, and Trixie

TECH TALK

A GLOSSARY OF COMPUTER ANIMATION TERMS

MODELING

All objects and characters are "modeled" in three dimensions within the computer to create a complete 3D description of their shape. Sets and furnishings are modeled with computer-aided design systems. Characters are modeled not just to describe their shape, but the movement of those shapes as well. This allows them to flex, stretch, and bend. Most characters have an underlying skeleton to allow fully articulated motion of joints and limbs.

AVARS

These are "articulated variables" within a model which can be controlled by an animator. For example, the angle at which Buzz bends his right elbow is one of several thousand avars created for the models in *Toy Story*.

DIGITIZE

All models are entered into the system through computer-aided design software. For more complicated models (such as human faces), actual clay sculpts were created and then 3D-scanned or digitized to convert them into computer-readable models.

PIXEL (ABBREVIATION FOR PICTURE ELEMENT)

All images for *Toy Story* are created and stored digitally. They are stored as a rectangular array of "pixels" (or picture elements), with each containing the color of the image at that point. Each finished frame of film requires 5MB (megabytes) of storage. On the average movie screen, a pixel is a square roughly a quarter inch per side.

RESOLUTION

The resolution of a digital image refers to the number of pixels stored. For *Toy Story*, the resolution is typically 1536 x 922 pixels.

RENDERING

The process of creating the final detail and color of an image. This involves collecting and combining data pertaining to each image. The computer assigned to render a frame starts by collecting scene descriptions, including the shape of all the objects (models), their poses (animation), surface descriptions (shaders), and lighting. The final image is then computed by determining the color of the object visible at each pixel.

SHADERS

These are computer programs for describing or defining surface appearance (such as brass, hardwood, wallpaper patterns). Shaders include information about color, texture, reflectivity, and bumpiness. Each shader informs the renderer as to how the various surfaces will reflect light.

TEXTURE MAPS

Many surface appearances are best described using pictures or images (which can be scanned in or painted). For example, the decals on Buzz include graphics designed in the art department. The curtain fabric in Andy's room was created by scanning a piece of real cloth. The dirt on Sid's desk is also painted. Each of these images is a texture map which is incorporated into the overall surface shader to control the color, reflectivity, and bumpiness of the surface. A texture map is a component of a shader.

UNWRAP

Much like unwrapping a birthday present and flattening the paper onto a flat surface. Pixar's art department uses a computer painting system to create texture maps and background images. Some texture maps are painted as flat images (or "flats") and projected onto a surface. Others are painted directly onto views of the three-dimensional surface.

CREATING *TOY STORY*

05

Everything you see in *Toy Story* exists in virtual space. From a pelting rainstorm to a beautiful sunset, a blade of grass to the 1.2 million leaves on the trees in Andy's neighborhood, the telephone poles, the gravel sidewalks, and the flicker of a burning match.

The process of computer animation is similar and, at the same time, very different from traditional animation. There are ten basic stages to creating each textured image: storyboards, editorial, production design, modeling, layout, animation, shading, lighting, rendering, and film recording. "It's like a giant animation factory," explains production supervisor Karen Robert Jackson. "Every frame must be approved in one stage before it can move down the pipeline to the next."

Like other animated films, artists begin with hand-drawn storyboards and then cut them together into story reels, putting actors' dialogue or scratch dialogue up against them. The story reels evolve into a patchwork quilt of storyboard drawings, pencil tests, or intermediary polygons, as well as final rendered imagery. Since most of Pixar's work is done digitally on various computers, editors Robert

Gordon and Lee Unkrich found video the most convenient medium to work in at this stage of the process.

Once the story reels are approved, they go to the art department, where art director Ralph Eggleston determines the overall lighting and color scheme for each sequence.

All animated objects and characters are modeled in three dimensions within the computer to create a complete 3D description of their shape. In all, some 2,000 models had to be crafted for *Toy Story*. Most character models have an underlying skeleton that allow fully articulated motion of joints and limbs. "Modelers are like digital-age marionette makers. We attach hundreds of interconnected strings that the animators can manipulate," explains animation scientist and modeler Eben Ostby. There are 800 separate avars (animation controls) on Buzz. For some of the more organic characters (anything involving skin), clay sculptures were built and then digitally scanned into the computer.

Sets and furnishings are modeled with computer-aided design systems. "Model packets," similar to an architect's blueprint, take into account the size and shape of every object in relation to everything else in the created world. "To our way of thinking, we build real sets," explains modeler Damir Frkovic. "They just happen to exist in virtual space instead of physical space. You've got to keep that live-action outlook if you want this to look like an actual working place, and not some perfect hermetically sealed illustration."

The layout department is responsible for the basic blocking of scenes and formulation of camera moves. "If you took a live-action director of photography and sawed him in half, we'd be the part that worries about the cameras," comments supervising layout artist Craig Good. "We do camera moves that could happen in real life with real cameras – everything from close-up, medium and wide shots, to tracking shots using dollies and cranes." Except in the world of computer animation there are no real cameras, only simulated cameras that have virtually no restraints.

But Good says he and lead layout artist Ewan Johnson followed established film grammar and avoided computer graphic gimmicks such as "delirious flybys" and "infinite tunnel shots."

The layout team deliberately borrowed shots from live-action directors, naming their cameras accordingly. "We have a Sir Kenneth Branagh-cam shot for the way the camera circled around in *Mary Shelley's Frankenstein* (1994)," observes Good. "It's a point in the film where the other toys think that Woody has deliberately pushed Buzz out of the window and they all attack him."

When animators receive a shot from layout, the shapes are represented by rough polygon shapes (polys) or by wire-frame figures. This simplified view of the character allows the computer to work faster and the animator to focus solely on the acting. "All you're left with to get across your meaning is movement and timing, which is fine, because that's the essence of animation," says directing animator Rich Quade.

Once a shot is animated, it goes into shading, lighting and, finally, full color rendering, where it is imbued with shadows and gorgeous lighting effects. For example, there is a brass shader, a hardwood floor shader, and an Andy's-room-wallpaper shader. The purpose of each shader is to inform the renderer about how various surfaces reflect light. The paint department then takes these computer-perfect surfaces and gives them wear and tear, dirt and grime.

07

06

Many surface appearances are best described in the computer using pictures. The decals on Buzz for example, include graphics designed by the art department. The weave of the comforter on Andy's bed was actually created by scanning a piece of real cloth. And the hallway carpet in Sid's house is lifted right out of Stanley Kubrick's *The Shining* (1980). Each of these images is used as a "texture map." More than 2,000 of these maps were painted for *Toy Story*.

The most dramatic visual transformation of a shot occurs in final lighting. It is here that the lighting crew paints the mood and ambiance of a shot using every imaginable lighting source that a live-action filmmaking crew might use – including the sun and the moon. "Except we can make our sun come out whenever we want it to," says lighting supervisor Galyn Susman. Nor does the lighting crew have to contend with heavy equipment, power plugs, or gels. Everything is controlled with a computerized menu system.

"We have key-lights, back-light, and rim lights," adds lighting supervisor Sharon Calahan. "We can put our shadows anywhere we want them, and we even have the ability to isolate lights to shine only on a particular character or object. In one shot, we have five lights shining just on Mr. Potato Head's ear."

"We've never done lighting like this before," says supervising technical director Bill Reeves. "The typical computer graphics scene uses diffuse, office light or has spotlights bouncing everywhere. We have dramatic moody lights in Sid's room, lens flares, flashlights, and bright sun. In one sequence we have a rainstorm with dark gray skies. A few shots later, light streams through the window."

The process of creating the final detail and color of an image is called rendering. The computer assigned to render a frame starts by collecting a complete scene description, including the shape of all objects (models), their poses (animation), surface descriptions (shaders) and lighting. The computer then computes the final images by determining the color of the object visible at each pixel. It took over 800,000-plus machine hours to render the final elements using Sun SPARCstation processors – running 24 hours a day in a special room appropriately named the "Sun Farm."

The final step in the process is the recording of these images onto film. ■

06. Bo Peep's sheep – Billy, Goat, and Gruff

07. Bo Peep, always ready to spring into action in *Toy Story 4*

08. Wise-cracking Hamm, the piggy bank

09. Rex, a dinosaur full of insecurity

09

08

HOOK-UP
COMES OFF

-GAMES IN ONE TRAILER.

GAPS IN THE SKIRT.

Concept art: Detail of a carnival attraction

TOY STORY EASTER EGGS, IN-JOKES, AND TRIVIA!

The team at Pixar could never resist in-jokes and references for moviegoers who are in the know. Here are some things to look out for...

TOY STORY

Release / November 22, 1995
Director / John Lasseter
Worldwide Box Office / $373.6 million

1
Many of the books on the shelf in Andy's bedroom are names of Pixar's short films, including "Adventures of Andre and Wally B." and "Knick Knack." Some of the book authors are named after Pixar staff.

2
"Julie MacBarfle has cooties" is written on Sid's backpack and refers to one of the movie's editors Julie MacDonald.

3
The gas station that Andy's mom stops at is called "Dinoco," which can also be seen in the Pixar film *Cars* as the oil company run by Tex Dinoco, and the sponsor of the Piston Cup.

4
The moving company logo seen on the side of the truck is named "Eggman Movers," which is named for Ralph Eggleston, the art director. His nickname with fellow crewmembers is "Eggman."

5
When Woody is sitting on the bed talking with Slinky Dog, there is a drawing of him on the wall behind them. This is actually an early sketch of the Woody character.

6
When Buzz stands on the end of the bed to prove to Woody that he really can fly, a large Mickey Mouse wristwatch can be seen on the wall.

7
The Green Army Men speak into the listening end of the one-way baby monitor.

8
Pizza Planet was originally going to be called Pizza Putt, which is a combination of a pizzeria and miniature golf course.

9
On Sid's desk in his bedroom you can see a can of Dr. Catmull's Old Fashioned Root Beer soda. Dr. Ed Catmull is a co-founder of Pixar Animation Studios.

10
The wallpaper in Andy's room can also be seen in *Monsters, Inc.* when the chameleon-like creature Randall has to copy the camouflage patterns during the training sequence.

TOY STORY 2

Release / November 24, 1999
Director / John Lasseter
Worldwide Box Office / $497.4 million

11
● In the opening sequence, Buzz Lightyear lands on an alien planet. This is actually the modified Ant Island cracked riverbed location from *A Bug's Life*.

12
● In her first shot, Mrs. Potato Head is reading an *A Bug's Life* book to the Little Tikes.

13
● Andy's cowboy camp T-shirt is from the "Triple R Ranch." This is the name of the ranch from the "Sid and Marty" TV series on *The Mickey Mouse Club*.

14
● The dog collar on a table at the yard sale originally appeared as the center ring in P.T. Flea's Circus in *A Bug's Life*.

15
● The painting over the couch in Al McWhiggin's living room is an abstract painting of characters from *A Bug's Life*.

16
● When the piggy bank toy, Hamm, is flipping through the TV channels, all the images are from Pixar commercials and short films.

17
● Characters that were storyboarded, but are not in the movie include:
- The New Yorkers
- Senorita Cactus
- Jack Rabbit
- Snake Eyed Sam and the Bandits
- Fluffy the Bear
- Pizza Planet Driver
- Sid

18
● *A Bug's Life* toys can be seen on the shelves in Al's Toy Barn.

19
● The cleaner who comes to repair Woody is Geri, star of Pixar's short film *Geri's Game*. His toolbox even has a drawer full of chess pieces.

20
● At the airport, you can hear some P.A. announcements. One is for "Leon Critch." This refers to co-director Lee Unkrich, whose name is often mispronounced as "Leon Critch."

21
● On the toys' journey to Al's Toy Barn, Buzz chops through some shrubs. If you look closely, you can see Heimlich from *A Bug's Life* climbing a branch.

22
● Al's Toy Barn is located at 1001 W. Cutting Blvd. In real life, this is Pixar's address!

23
● 29,357 story panels were drawn, delivered, and shot in Editorial for *Toy Story 2*.

24
● Al has a wall calendar in his office with a drawing of an early design for his car.

25
● 42 pencil sharpeners gave their lives to make this film.

26
● There are 3,693 shaders (computer programs used for shading) in *Toy Story 2*. That's about equal to the numbers in the original *Toy Story* and *A Bug's Life* combined.

27
● Hamm is carrying over $6 in change.

28
● There are 2,982 superballs in the superball shots in Al's Toy Barn.

29
● There are nearly 35,000 texture maps (an image applied/ mapped to the surface of a shape or polygon) in *Toy Story 2* that occupy nearly 40 GB of disk space.

30
● Al has 130,000 hairs on his head. 1,500 of these are used for his combover.

31
● 3,405,759 hairs comprise Buster's fur.

32
● Emily has posters and records from the rock group "The Lemurs" in her room. Earlier in the movie, Al passes up buying an 8-Track tape of "The Lemurs: Greatest Hits" at the yard sale.

33
● There are over 70 different package designs in Al's Toy Barn, including such gems as "Baby Drool-a-lot," "DMV Agitation," and "My Little Mongrel."

34
● The model for the Prospector's head began as Al's head.

35
● Over 4,000 videotapes were generated for *Toy Story 2*. This adds up to 10,800,000 feet of videotape.

36
● It took over a month to digitally paint Al's car.

37
● There are roughly 2,400,000 individual particles of dust on Andy's shelf at the start of the film.

38
● There are 811 new designs in *Toy Story 2*.

39
● There are 29 locations visited in *Toy Story 2*.

40
● Jessie and Woody share the same buttons and belts.

41
● The Prospector's handkerchief is the same as Woody's shirt fabric.

TOY STORY 2

42
● The shortest shader is 19 lines of compiled code; the longest is nearly 25,000 lines.

43
● Rex is an aspiring space ranger.

44
● Tour Guide Barbie is bi-lingual.

45
● Jessie was originally cast as a common desert plant named Senorita Cactus.

46
● There are roughly 4,500,000 particles of dust under Emily's bed.

47
● Wheezy coughs up more than 100,000 individual dust particles over the span of the film as he tries to better his "condition."

48
● The model number on the camera flash in the conveyor belt sequence is 112499 – a reference to November 24, 1999, *Toy Story 2*'s release date.

49
● *Toy Story 2* used 1,792 more story panels than *A Bug's Life*.

50
● Wheezy's body is painted with over 60 illustrations.

51
● The Pizza Planet Truck had to be repainted to make it look rustier and dirtier than in the original *Toy Story*.

52
● All of the graphics in the Woody's Roundup collection took over a year to complete.

53
● 16 different people worked on building the Al McWhiggin model. This does not include the people who worked on Al's shading, hair, or fixes.

54
● The conveyor belt system is composed of 2,070 separate pieces of track. The length from start to end is 2.7 miles, but the total length of conveyor belt is actually 5.4 miles, going from start to end and then around back to the start.

55
● The most animation produced in one week of production was 5 minutes and 42 seconds.

56
● 1,034 models were built and are visible in *Toy Story 2*.

57
● There are more than 10,000 texture maps created for the human characters alone.

TOY STORY 3

Release / June 18, 2010
Director / Lee Unkrich
Worldwide Box Office / $1.067 billion

58

● *Toy Story 3* Producer Darla K. Anderson is the namesake for the character Darla in *Finding Nemo*.

59

● Director Lee Unkrich performs one line in the movie, as the voice of the Jack-in-the-Box character who says, "New Toys!" when Woody, Buzz, and the gang first arrive at Sunnyside.

60

● On January 15, 2010, the final day for many of the 58-person animation crew, director Lee Unkrich led a mini-marching band through the studio, composed of several drummers, two giant monkeys, and a Yeti.

61

● 17 animators on *Toy Story 3* also worked on animation for *Toy Story 2*. Four animators worked on the animation for all three *Toy Story* films.

62

● 92,854 storyboards were drawn over the course of the film.

63

● There are 302 characters in *Toy Story 3*.

64

● For its release, *Toy Story 3* was dubbed into 43 different languages. 12 of these also include international language visual inserts (where any written language seen in the film is also translated).

65

● 68 babies were born to Pixar employees during the production of *Toy Story 3*. Known internally as "Production Babies," all 68 are listed during the film's end credits.

66

● There are 1,484,437 monkeys in the barrel that is dropped when Hamm presses the "Death by Monkeys" button in the film's opening sequence.

67

● Members of the effects team were sent on a research trip to a garbage dump. However, they went to the wrong one, and the manager of the dump was confused by their disappointment that there was no shredder or incinerator for them to study.

68

● The number 95, on the side of the train in the opening sequence, is a reference to 1995, the year the original *Toy Story* was released.

69

● The drawings of Bonnie's toys that are taped to the walls of her bedroom in the epilogue were drawn by director Lee Unkrich's children, Hannah, Alice, and Max.

70

● The longest shot in the film, in which Lotso attempts to convince Buzz why some toys need to stay in Sunnyside Daycare's Caterpillar Room, contained 38 feet of continuous animation.

71

● Director Lee Unkrich edited the first two *Toy Story* films, and co-directed *Toy Story 2*. He also served as a film editor on *Toy Story 3*.

TOY STORY 3

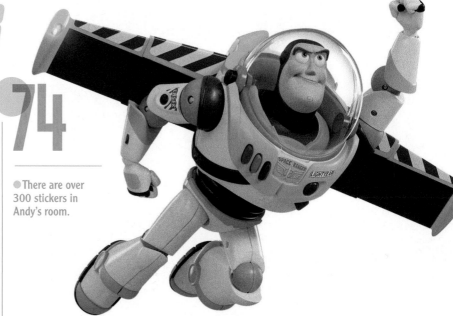

72

● When Lotso's gang are gambling in the vending machine at Sunnyside, they are placing bets with Re-Volting batteries, which was the sponsor of racer 84 in *Cars*.

73

● The license plate number A113 is a reference to John Lasseter, Brad Bird, Pete Docter, and Andrew Stanton's former classroom at CalArts, and makes an appearance in every Pixar film.

74

● There are over 300 stickers in Andy's room.

75

● The pins on the map in Andy's room correspond to the hometowns of *Toy Story 3* production staff.

76

● A few pieces of art hanging on the walls in Andy's room were actually created by *Toy Story 3* art coordinator Erin Magill when she was in high school.

77

● Andy has a banner hanging on one of the walls in his room that reads "P.U." P.U. stands for Pixar University, a professional-development program for Pixar employees.

78

● Above Andy's closet is a street sign for West Cutting Boulevard, the street on which Pixar's original headquarters were based.

79

● Sid makes a cameo in *Toy Story 3*, wearing his signature skull T-shirt. Sid is once again voiced by Erik Von Detten.

80

● *Toy Story 3* contains several references to Lee Unkrich's favorite film, *The Shining*.

81

● The group of toys hiding under the shelving unit before the young children come racing into Sunnyside are inspired by Pixar's short film, *Tin Toy*, in which a small toy is terrorized by an infant.

82

● Sunnyside Daycare is sprinkled with toy versions of familiar faces of past Pixar characters, including Lightning McQueen (*Cars*) and Mr. Ray (*Finding Nemo*).

83

● One of the toys in Bonnie's room is a bunny-like stuffed animal. This is Totoro, from Hayao Miyazaki's film *My Neighbor Totoro*.

84

● The troll dolls seen at Sunnyside Daycare are wearing handmade felt clothes of the same design as those made by Lee Unkrich's wife, Laura, for her own troll dolls as a child.

85

● In honor of *Toy Story 3*, LEGO created a six-foot-six-inch-tall version of Woody that weighed 80 pounds, built from more than 17,200 bricks.

86

● ...and LEGO also created a five-foot-three version of Buzz that weighed 120 pounds, made from 25,000 LEGO bricks. Both models now have a permanent home at Pixar.

87
● Woody is 15.18 inches tall without his hat, and 15.93 inches tall with his hat on.

88
● Woody has 229 animation avars in his face. Avars, short for animation variables, are the points of movement, which animators manipulate to create a character's physical performance.

89
● The batteries used to power Buzz Lightyear are from BnL (Buy n Large), the mega-corporation featured in WALL•E.

90
● Roughly 1.8 million Woodys could fit inside the volume of fire and smoke in the incinerator towards the end of *Toy Story 3*.

91
● Buzz is 11.43 inches tall without his helmet, and 11.80 inches with it. Buzz has 215 animation avars in his face.

92
● To represent the different stages of Lotso's life, the *Toy Story 3* character team created different versions of the plush bear: new, new dirty, new filthy, new wet, new soaked, standard, and standard filthy.

93
● In Pixar's *Up*, Lots-o'-Huggin' Bear (Lotso) can be seen sitting on the floor of a little girl's bedroom as Carl's house flies past her window.

94
● Lotso has 3,473,271 individual hairs organized in several layers of different length and thickness.

95
● Ken wears 21 different outfits in the movie.

96
● The version of Ken used in *Toy Story 3* was modeled after "Animal Lovin' Ken" from 1988.

97
● The version of Barbie used in *Toy Story 3* was modeled after the "Great Shape Barbie" that was first produced in 1983.

98
● The character of Andy is voiced by actor John Morris, who voices Andy in all of the films to date.

99
● In *Toy Story 3*, Andy is preparing to leave for college. In real life, John Morris was 26 years old.

100
● Andy was 8 years old in *Toy Story* and *Toy Story 2*. In *Toy Story 3*, he was 17 years old.

TOY STORY 4

Release / June 21, 2019
Director / Josh Cooley

101

● Tom Hanks (Woody) and Tim Allen (Buzz) both admitted they found the ending of the film extremely emotional. Hanks said that he had to turn away from the crew while he was recording.

102

● Voice actor Don Rickles (Mr. Potato Head) sadly passed away in April 2017. His part in *Toy Story 4* is made up from archived recordings of his voice from previous *Toy Story* projects.

103

● Duke Caboom officially makes his debut in *Toy Story 4* – but you can actually see a Duke Caboom toy lying in Jack-Jack's crib in the *Incredibles 2* movie.

104

● When Woody and Bo meet Duke Caboom, a whole side story was created for the crowd in the background. However, the side story was so absorbing that it was toned down to make it less distracting.

105

● Tom Hanks and Tim Allen completed work on the film on January 30, 2019.

106

● The only cast members to have appeared in all four *Toy Story* films are Tom Hanks (Woody), Tim Allen (Buzz), Wallace Shawn (Rex), John Ratzenberger (Hamm), Jeff Pidgeon (Aliens), and Laurie Metcalf (Mrs. Davis).

107

● This film is Keanu Reeves' first animated film.

108

● The street number for the Second Chance antiques store (1200) is the same as Pixar Animation Studios.

109

● Director Josh Cooley has voice-acted in several other Pixar films, including as Jangles the clown in *Inside Out* and Omega the dog in *Up*.

110

● Forky has "Bonnie" written on his feet – similar to how Buzz and Woody had "Andy" written on theirs.

111

● The film was released in theaters on June 21, 2019, in RealD 3D, Dolby Cinema, and IMAX 3D.

112

● Madeleine McGraw (Bonnie) made her film debut as McKenna in Academy Award®-nominated film *American Sniper* when she was just six years old, and she was 10 years old when she voiced Bonnie.

Disney · PIXAR

TOY STORY 4

"Everything is going to be okay!"

Forky

CINEMAS SOON

DISNEY LIBRARY

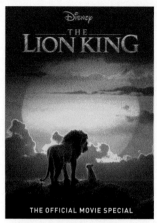

DISNEY DUMBO
THE OFFICIAL MOVIE SPECIAL

DISNEY THE LION KING
THE OFFICIAL MOVIE SPECIAL
(JULY 2019)

DISNEY FROZEN 2
THE OFFICIAL MOVIE SPECIAL
(OCTOBER 2019)

MARVEL LIBRARY

X-MEN
DAYS OF FUTURE PAST

NOVELS
- **ANT-MAN** NATURAL ENEMY
- **AVENGERS** EVERYBODY WANTS TO RULE THE WORLD
- **AVENGERS** INFINITY
- **BLACK PANTHER** WHO IS THE BLACK PANTHER?
- **CAPTAIN MARVEL** LIBERATION RUN
- **CIVIL WAR**
- **DEADPOOL** PAWS
- **SPIDER-MAN** FOREVER YOUNG
- **SPIDER-MAN** HOSTILE TAKEOVER
- **SPIDER-MAN** KRAVEN'S LAST HUNT
- **THANOS** DEATH SENTENCE
- **VENOM** LETHAL PROTECTOR
- **X-MEN** DAYS OF FUTURE PAST
- **X-MEN** THE DARK PHOENIX SAGA

THE ART OF IRON MAN
10TH ANNIVERSARY EDITION

ARTBOOKS
- **MARVEL'S SPIDER-MAN** THE ART OF THE GAME
- **MARVEL: CONQUEST OF CHAMPIONS** THE ART OF THE BATTLEREALM
- **SPIDER-MAN: INTO THE SPIDERVERSE**

MOVIE SPECIALS
- **MARVEL STUDIOS' AVENGERS: ENDGAME**
- **MARVEL STUDIOS' AVENGERS: INFINITY WAR**
- **MARVEL STUDIOS' BLACK PANTHER (COMPANION)**
- **MARVEL STUDIOS' BLACK PANTHER (SPECIAL)**
- **MARVEL STUDIOS' CAPTAIN MARVEL**
- **MARVEL STUDIOS: THE FIRST TEN YEARS**
- **MARVEL STUDIOS' THOR: RAGNAROK**

- **SPIDER-MAN: INTO THE SPIDERVERSE**

STAR WARS LIBRARY

- **ROGUE ONE: A STAR WARS STORY** THE OFFICIAL COLLECTOR'S EDITION
- **ROGUE ONE: A STAR WARS STORY** THE OFFICIAL MISSION DEBRIEF
- **STAR WARS: THE LAST JEDI** THE OFFICIAL COLLECTOR'S EDITION
- **STAR WARS: THE LAST JEDI** THE OFFICIAL MOVIE COMPANION
- **STAR WARS: THE LAST JEDI** THE ULTIMATE GUIDE

- **SOLO: A STAR WARS STORY** THE OFFICIAL COLLECTOR'S EDITION
- **SOLO: A STAR WARS STORY** THE ULTIMATE GUIDE
- **THE BEST OF STAR WARS INSIDER** VOLUME 1
- **THE BEST OF STAR WARS INSIDER** VOLUME 2
- **THE BEST OF STAR WARS INSIDER** VOLUME 3
- **THE BEST OF STAR WARS INSIDER** VOLUME 4

- **STAR WARS:** LORDS OF THE SITH
- **STAR WARS:** HEROES OF THE FORCE
- **STAR WARS:** ICONS OF THE GALAXY
- **STAR WARS:** THE SAGA BEGINS
- **STAR WARS INSIDER** THE ORIGINAL TRILOGY
- **STAR WARS:** ROGUES, SCOUNDRELS AND BOUNTY HUNTERS (SEPTEMBER 2019)

STAR WARS INSIDER
THE SAGA BEGINS

STAR WARS INSIDER
THE ORIGINAL TRILOGY